# Voices

# *Voices*

Patrice Carolyn Forrester

RESOURCE *Publications* · Eugene, Oregon

VOICES

Resource Publications
An Imprint of Wipf and Stock Publishers
199 W. 8th Ave., Suite 3
Eugene, OR 97401

www.wipfandstock.com

PAPERBACK ISBN: 978-1-4982-8194-2
HARDCOVER ISBN: 978-1-4982-8196-6
EBOOK ISBN: 978-1-4982-8195-9

Manufactured in the U.S.A.

For my mother—her strength and love
For all those crying out for freedom and restoration

# Contents

*Introduction* | ix

Voices | 1
The Education of Sally Plummer | 2
American History 101 | 6
Social Worker | 7
Grandma Laura | 8
Revolutionary Statement:
I am Black and Beautiful | 9
Legacy | 11
Inca | 12
Lord Rawdon's Men | 13
Victory! | 14
War Work | 16
Congo | 17
Princess | 18
Testimony | 21
Migrant Mother | 22
Ora Et Labora | 23
Into Light | 24

*Notes on Selected Poems* | 25
*Bibliography* | 29

# Introduction

These poems tell the stories of great oppression, pride, pain, and resilience. As I reflected on the lives of other women in history and our current day, stories began to form in my imagination about their lives. I began to write their stories based on the historical record and my own observations in the form of narrative poems.

The poems gathered here present the experiences of those who are all too easily ignored and marginalized due to their race, class, ethnicity, or gender. The poems at the beginning of this collection give voice to black women, a group that has been vilified, honored, and discounted. Additional poems in this collection present a variety of women's voices who express the sexual exploitation of women in war and peacetime, as well as the healing that comes through connections with others and a sense of hope for the future.

Even as these poems shed light on the stories of particular people and events, I hope that you will look to find your own story as you reflect on the lives of those portrayed here. May you experience the freedom and healing that can come from authentically using your own unique voice.

# Voices

We refuse
To crush our hearts
To chain our souls

We dream of freedom
We dream of freedom

We dream
Of voices
One day
Released

Refusing to be
Silenced

# The Education of Sally Plummer

*South Carolina Circa 1867*

### I

I was reared on Marsden Bluff
As long as I can remember
Worked up at the Big House
Hated it
Mistress always calling
Never resting

Never knew Mama
Sold her off when I was just a little girl
Way down South
Miz Clary said
I used to ask Miz Clary what Mama was like
Miz Clary would smile
Said I looked just like her
Big brown eyes
Wide smile
That made me smile
It made me sad too

### II

As I worked in the Big House
I walked by young massa
As he read his book for reading lessons
I saw the words
He wrote down
I liked to hear him read
I began to memorize the words
Practiced writing them in the ground when I was alone

I began to recognize some of the words young massa wrote
As I dusted the books in the study
Young massa and Mistress
Would always say
"Sally sure is dumb"
Laughing
As I cleaned
During lessons
They never saw
I was playing dumb
So I could learn to read


## III

Soon as Massa came home from the War
Yankees started following
Told us that we slaves were free
We were even free to read
But Massa still believed that we were slaves
Broke a whip across any that
Broke the old slave rule
Yankees kept telling us that we were free
They would protect our freedom by force if necessary
We would learn from Yankee teachers coming down
Massa couldn't break no whip across no one after that


## IV

Miz Ellen was our teacher
She was a single white woman
From Up North
She talked real nasal like her nose was plugged up
I got to learn more words for what I felt on the inside
It was like those words let my voice rise

## V

Over time, I began to read so well
Miz Ellen said I could help teach the
Beginning students
Miz Clary beamed at me every morning I went to school
She said, "Yo mama sho would be proud."

## VI

I started writing in a book Miz Ellen gave me
A journal
She said I could practice writing
Share my thoughts within its pages
I liked writing in the book
It made my heart light
I sometimes forgot I lived on Marsden Bluff
As I wrote everything down
When I wrote I was free

## VII

A year later, I became a teacher on the Sea Islands
Miz Ellen said they needed teachers
To continue the work
Of Freedom
She gave me a letter
Of recommendation

## VIII

Miz Clary is the closest thing I have to a Mama
Before I traveled off the plantation
She said
"God Bless the day you came out yo' Mama's womb. You free and you showin us
we is free."
Miz Clary placed her hand on my head in blessing
Tears stung her eyes
I hugged Miz Clary and told her I would visit
Miz Clary just nodded, "Yes, chile."


## IX

I teach
On an island of pain
The hope of
Freedom
Teaching our people
That we are free
Voices

Ringing Out Loud

# American History 101

*In memory of Ida B. Wells Barnett*

Unnamed
Unmarked
Unknown
At the Hands of
Persons Unknown

But for your voice
America
Could forget
Ropes Swaying
Bulging Black Necks
Roasted Corpses
Castrated Manhood

But your voice
Screams through the years
Not willing that anyone
Forget
Memories Shameful
Bodies Painful
American History 101

# Social Worker

*In memory of Anna Arnold Hedgeman*


In 1930s New York
Working with migrants newly arrived
Searching for work

I saw the Bronx Slave Market
Where white women would
Inspect black women like
Animals for sale
Maids for little or no pay

I headed Brooklyn's YWCA
Involved in protests
"Don't Buy Where You Can't Work"
In the midst of the Depression

I heard the resonant strains of Robeson
The syncopated rhymes of Langston
I knew my people intimately in Harlem
Rich Poor
In all their hues

Beautiful
Black
Just like Me

# Grandma Laura

## *Chicago, Illinois Circa 1958*

*In memory of Laura & L.D. Nelson*
*d. May 25, 1911*


One dark blue night
You were led
To your death
My uncle
Beside you
Hung
Over the North Canadian River

My mother rarely talks about you
Only in hushed tones
Gathered with family
Survivors

Your grave is not a place we visit
It burdens too much
Tragedies of the race

Oh!
How I wish I knew you
Apart from your death

# Revolutionary Statement:
# I Am Black and Beautiful

*Washington, DC Circa 1970*

I am black
Black is my pride
My ancestors
Africans transplanted
Slaves they named them
Forced to cut cane
Pick cotton
Plant rice

I am black
My great-grandparents freed
Educated children
Teachers
To the next generation

I am black
My grandparents re-enslaved
Fought for Freedom
Against
Lynching
Rape
Segregation

I am black
My parents liberated
Birthed a fire
Deep within me
In suburbs
In ghettoes
In towns

I am black
Black is beautiful

I am black
Beautiful
Like the ancestors
I resemble

# Legacy

I am the legacy
Of those who came before
I rise among the trees
Growing from the undergrowth
My leafy branches
Spread over the Earth
Sending out Light
I stand more firmly
To my roots
As I shoot up
To the sky

# Inca

*Peru Circa 1572*

Gold
Homage to the
Sun

Inca
Atahualpa

Gold
Homage to
Pizarro

Temples
Gold
Stolen
Burned
Buried

And I live
Not Spanish
Not Indio
Mestizo

Embracing both
And none
I am none

# Lord Rawdon's Men

## *New Jersey Circa 1776*

Redcoats
Destroy dark wooden tables
Stick silver black rifles
In my face

Redcoats
Shove
Shout
"Show us to the barn. You may be hidin' rebels there"

I open the rickety latch
Fear follows

One jumps
Another rips
Bodice
Tears

Hands spread
Over my
Limp body

My eyes see my mother
In heaven
Comforting
My body
No longer
Here
Below

# Victory!

## *Berlin, Germany Circa 1945*

May 1945
Liberation for most
Defeat for us

Hitler
In the grave

Bombs
Soar

Death
Rises

Walking
Tattered Streets

Battle-Worn Boys
Massacred Men

Wilted Women
Grown-Up Girls

Swiftly
Surely
Red Army
Soldiers
Revenge in their
Scarred Souls
March Victorious

Claim
Female
Bounty
Chained
Daily
To
Borrowed
Despoiled
Beds

Victory!
Hitler Kaput!

# War Work

*Bosnia-Herzegovina Circa 1995*

Taken
For work
They said

We would work
Nightly
Nightly

Our Bodies
Taken
Every Night

# Congo

*Circa 2004*

The Belgians came first
Bringing genocide
Cutting hands
On rubber plantations
Raped
Killed
All to subjugate
All to humiliate
All to terrorize
Congo

Now the soldiers come
The rebels come too
Bringing war
Cutting hands
In the diamond mines
Rape
Kill
All to subjugate
All to humiliate
All to terrorize
Congo

# Princess

## *Washington, DC 2010*

### I

They call me Princess
My real name Keisha

DC
Nation's Capital

Home
Nothin' but
Nights

Ma smokin' crack
Prostitutin'
Daddy locked up
Drug dealin'

### II

Kyle
He real fine
Light complected
Hazel eyes
He 25
I'm 12

Kyle
Take me to dinner
To McDonalds
Call me

Pretty
Smart
I love him

Kyle
Care
He protect me
He give
Me
Clothes
Money
I love him

## III

Now
I
Walk the track
For our money
Kyle say
"We make enough money, We go buy a nice big house"
Away from the Lights of the
City
I dream a lot
As I walk the track
Nights

## IV

One night
I come up short
I was too high
To notice

Kyle
Pull my ear
Punch my eye
Split my lip
Kick my nose
"You go out there and get me my money"


V

Daylight
I come back with our money
Kyle kiss me
Apologize
Take care of my bruises
I love him
We stay in bed till
Night

# Testimony

## *Iowa 2013*

I worked every day to feed my family
The Boss cornered me with his eyes
Salivating

One evening
Late
He pointed a brown shriveled nail
He planted his oily palms around me
He took me to his office
Lukewarm
Like his hands
"If you not nice to me, I get you fired"
I needed this job

You may say
I sold my body for a job
I say I saved my family
With my flesh
My four girls
Only have me
I needed that job

Now I speak
Before this judge
Before this jury
For my daughters

For me I did not care
For my daughters
I must stand
I must testify
For my daughters
Must live
Free

# Migrant Mother

## *California 2015*

In the fields I plant
Rubbing my hand against my wet face
I bend my knees in the hot sun

It will pay my daughter's school fee
It will pay our bills

In the fields I plant
While my husband
Plays with money
And girls

But my daughter
She will live
A life of
Freedom
I plant

# Ora et Labora

*Los Angeles, California 2016*

*Dedicated to Homeboy Industries*


We work
Side by side
Sworn enemies
But a year before

Strange how enemies
Become friends
While preparing meals
To serve others

Strange how we
Become
Undefended
Vulnerable
Receiving
The Gift
We each carry
Deep in our
Hearts

The
Healing
Answer to
Our
Prayers

# Into Light

Rough Rock
Demolished
Splintered
Scattered
Across this Earth

Diamond
Dark Dust
Tenderly Touched
Hands Communally Circle
Polishing
The luster appears
Gleaming
Bright
Light

Light
Showering
Illumination
On a world
Hidden in Darkness

I stand
Because
The sun always
Rises
Darkness cannot overcome
The
Everlasting Light

# Notes on Selected Poems

The Education of Sally Plummer takes place after the Civil War when black slaves were freed. At that time, many black people were eager to gain an education for themselves and their children. They wanted to be free not only in their bodies but in their minds as well.[1]

American History 101 is an ode to Ida B. Wells, a black journalist, newspaper editor, and leader in the US women's rights and civil rights movements in the late 19th and early 20th century. She is most notable for documenting the epidemic of lynching, the practice of executing people by extrajudicial mob action, which was largely used against black people after the abolition of slavery.[2]

Social Worker profiles scenes in the life of Anna Arnold Hedgeman, a black social worker, educator, politician, and human rights activist. In 1930's United States, an economic depression occurred that later came to be known as the Great Depression. At the time of the Great Depression, a corner of Prospect Avenue and 167th Street in NY City was termed the Bronx "slave market" where black women were picked up by wealthy women for temporary employment doing housework. Langston Hughes, a poet, and Paul Robeson, a singer, were famous black artists. Harlem, NY was a mecca of black cultural and political life, especially during the 1920's.[3]

Grandma Laura is written in the imagined voice of the granddaughter of Laura Nelson. Laura Nelson was a black female who was lynched along with her son L.D. Nelson by a white mob on May 25, 1911.[4]

---

1. Lerner, *Black Women*, 92–94.
2. Ibid., 196–199.
3. Sugrue, *Sweet Land*, 5–30.
4. Allen, *Notes*, 178–180.

The poem Revolutionary Statement: I am Black and Beautiful is set in the early 1970's when many black people began to take more pride in their heritage.[5]

Inca reflects on the conquest of the Inca, an indigenous people of Peru, by the Spaniards in the 16th century. Atahualpa was an Incan ruler who was killed by Spaniards under the leadership of Francisco Pizarro in 1533. In Incan religion, the sun god Inti was the most important. The Incas were goldsmith specialists, and the Spaniards lusted after the gold they saw in the Incan empire.[6]

Lord Rawdon's Men describes an incident in which a woman from New Jersey is raped by men under the command of Lord Rawdon, a British officer who fought against the American colonists in their War for Independence from Great Britain. In the Fall and Winter of 1776, many girls were raped by British soldiers in New Jersey and Staten Island.[7]

Victory! takes place in the waning days of World War II as armies from the East and West were nearing the city of Berlin in Germany to defeat its tyrannical regime led by Hitler that had killed millions of Jews and other people considered undesirable. Millions of women and girls in Berlin were raped by the invading armies, especially by the Russian army whose people had been brutalized, killed, and raped by invading German armies during the course of the war.[8]

In War Work, the voice of an anonymous woman details the sexual violence meted out to her and other Bosnian women during the Bosnian War. The Bosnian War occurred after the break-up of Yugoslavia in Eastern Europe and subsequent conflict between various ethnic groups such as the Serbians and Bosnian Muslims.[9]

5. Joseph, *Black Power*, 752–756.

6. Von Hagen, "The Incas," lines 1–268.

7. Norton, *Liberty's Daughters*, 202–203.

8. Hitchcock, *The Bitter Road*, 131–169.

9. Abu-Hamad, et al., *The Human Rights Watch*, 8–24.

Congo reflects on the ongoing war in the African nation of Congo which also involves the mass rape of Congolese women.[10]

Princess details the story of a young woman who becomes a prostitute. Currently, the age of entry into prostitution in the United States is about 12 years old. These US minors are considered domestic trafficking victims under US law.[11]

The poem Testimony focuses on the sexual harassment of women, including undocumented immigrant women, who work in US factories.[12]

Ora et Labora is a Latin phrase meaning Pray and Work. The poem Ora et Labora highlights Homeboy Industries, a gang intervention and reentry program in Los Angeles, California whose founder Father Greg Boyle is a Catholic priest. One of Homeboy Industry's social enterprises is Homegirl Café where young men and women learn to work with former gang rivals and gain important job skills in a supportive environment. [13]

10. Jones, *War is not Over*, 131–167.

11. Lloyd, *Girls*, 33–132.

12. Bauer and Ramírez, *Injustice*, 41–53.

13. Homeboy Industries, "Homegirl Café," 1-31.

# Bibliography

Abu-Hamad, Aziz, et al. *The Human Rights Watch Global Report on Women's Human Rights*. United States: Human Rights Watch, 1995.

Allen, James. "Notes on the Plates." In *Without Sanctuary: Lynching Photography in America*, 178–180. Santa Fe, NM: Twin Palms, 2000.

Bauer, Mary, and Mónica Ramírez. *Injustice on our Plates: Immigrant Women in the U.S. Food Industry*. Montgomery, AL: Southern Poverty Law Center, 2010.

Hitchcock, William I. *The Bitter Road to Freedom: The Human Cost of Allied Victory in World War II Europe*. New York: Free, 2008.

Homeboy Industries. "Home Girl Café and Catering." http://www.homeboyindustries.org/what-we-do/homegirl-cafe/welcome/.

Jones, Ann. *War is not Over When it's Over: Women Speak out From the Ruins of War*. New New York: Metropolitan, 2010.

Joseph, Peniel E. "The Black Power Movement: A State of the Field." *The Journal of American History* 96, no. 3 (2009) 751–776.

Lerner, Gerda, ed. *Black Women in White America: A Documentary History*. New York: Vintage, 1972.

Lloyd, Rachel. *Girls Like Us: Fighting for a World Where Girls are Not for Sale, an Activist Finds Her Calling and Heals Herself*. New York: HarperCollins, 2011.

Norton, Mary Beth. *Liberty's Daughters: The Revolutionary Experience of American Women, 1750–1800*. Ithaca, NY: Cornell University Press, 1980.

Von Hagen, Victor W. "The Incas." http://www.latinamericanstudies.org/incas/collier.htm.

www.ingramcontent.com/pod-product-compliance
Lightning Source LLC
Chambersburg PA
CBHW060704280326
41933CB00012B/2303